TAMING TANTRUMS

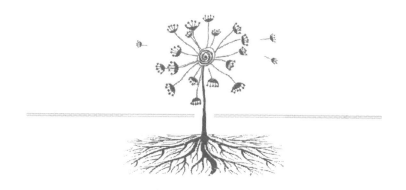

WENDY BERTAGNOLE

The information in this eBook is based on personal experience and anecdotal evidence. Although the author has made every reasonable attempt to achieve complete accuracy of the content in this book, she assumes no responsibility for errors or omissions. This information is to be used at your own risk. Every situation is different and will not be an exact replica of the examples given in this eBook. The author cannot guarantee results or any specific outcomes as a result of using the methods outlined in the book. This work is not written or endorsed by any other person, company, or product recommended in the material.

CONTENTS

INTRODUCTION

I set out to be the most perfect mom ever, little did I know just how impossible that task would be to achieve. I just knew I wouldn't scream and yell, that I would talk through everything with my kids and that we would have blissful moments filled with laughter and joy every day. Walks to the park would be like a scene in a movie, our interactions would be warm and gentle, and our smiles would reflect the love we all felt for each other.

Then I became a mother.

With my first child, I really did love motherhood. Most days were filled with new adventures, laughter, love, and the occasional tears that we would work through together. It was **almost** as perfect as I had imagined. I held tight to my own vision of motherhood, I didn't care too much about living up to what other's thought, and didn't go to many people for advice. I didn't have to. I felt like I had it all under control…well mostly.

Except at night, when I became a human pacifier, I was kicked out of my own bed and had to sleep in a guest bed with my son. Unless we were attached, he wouldn't sleep, and without sleep I can't function. We co-slept until he was two, but I didn't tell many people, because of the shame I felt about my "dark secret" that threatened my "perfect mom status". When other moms were "getting their kids to sleep at 3 months," mine was still clinging to me every moment of the night. I was wearing down, but I put on a game face and played my role well. Little did I know, that was only the tip of the iceberg.

When I had my second child, a shift began to take place, one I wouldn't recognize for many years. The picture I had of the "perfect mom" changed. It started to look less like me, and more like a role I played to look more like a posed social media post; cute kid, dressed to a T, and acting like a "well behaved kid." I started listening to and believing more in the parenting advice of others than my own parenting instincts. My parenting approach had evolved into a reflection of what other people told me was right: upholding a certain image, and keeping it all together. At least on the outside.

Inside the home we were a mess. My youngest son would cry at the drop of a hat. My oldest son would whine to get the attention he missed when he was an only child. I felt like I was walking on eggshells, breaking any and all parenting rules, just to avoid another meltdown. My kids were emotional, and I couldn't do anything to change it.

I tried ignoring it.

I tried yelling over it.

I tried being more consistent.

I tried being more patient.

I tried counting to ten before responding.

But NOTHING worked.

I was exhausted and felt like I was failing my children. How could I have children whose behavior I couldn't get under control? Was it a phase? Was it my own hormones? Would it pass? Or was I just a horrible mom?

The latter option was what felt most true at the time. Everyone else around me seemed to do it all with ease, and here I was struggling every day to make it through without losing my mind.

What others couldn't see behind the well-dressed kids and the good front I played in public, was the daily chaos I lived and struggled with each day. The constant yelling (from me and my kids). Daily, and often hourly tantrums (from me and my kids).

Then I had a third child. And that's when I broke.

I felt out of control. Nothing I tried was working. I felt like a complete failure. I gave up.

I had no idea where I went wrong or WHY! I felt alone and exhausted.

That social media picture of the perfect mom I tried so hard to become, felt so far from our reality. My textbook education had proven to not be enough. Typical mom strategies were failing me. I wanted to quit.

That year I started a desperate search to understand why these tantrums were happening. How I could be more patient. And how to stop "waiting for a phase" to be over or "hoping for the best" with my kids. I wanted to be intentional and feel more peace in my home, but I had no clue how.

That was five years ago. Things are different now. Drawing ideas from the dozens of books I have read, my master's degree in special education, and trying them in my own home over the years, I have come up with a mindset shift, a different way of approaching my children's behavior, that keeps even the most extreme tantrums and behaviors at a minimum. It's also the way I've returned to a position of truly loving motherhood, showing up as the mom I want to be, and feeling the daily joy of living my own parenting dream.

I have developed simple and powerful concepts that have transformed my life as a parent, my connection with my kids, and my approach to behavior in general. Over the past two years I've had the privilege of sharing these ideas with thousands of other moms across the globe through online courses. Students who have learned these concepts as I teach them say things such as:

"To me, it was a mental relief to start approaching my child in this fashion. It gave me new energy to help my child." –Heather H.

"This was the missing piece I have been looking for!" –Krystle L.

"She gave me a perspective and a new way of addressing the same old problem/challenge." --McCall N.

That's what I share with you here, with all the empathy of a mom who "gets" what you are going through. One who has been through the sleepless nights feeling like a horrible parent, one who has walked shamelessly through the grocery store, with my screaming kid in hand, avoiding the judgmental glances from strangers, one who is still in the thick of the parenting mess, and who truly understands it's frustrations.

I don't offer a quick fix, or even a way to banish tantrums forever. Those "magic fixes" don't last, and trying to implement them will only make things worse. Tantrums will still happen. We all have them at times. Knowing how to handle them and why they happen, and even how to avoid a good portion of them, is what I can offer. That, my friend, is what I share here.

Parenting doesn't need to be exhausting. It will rarely be perfect, but you have the power to make it more fun, fulfilling, and productive for both you and your children. It truly can be everything you imagined it would be. So dust off that picture of the mom you originally set out to be. The unpolluted, unashamed, and wonderful parent you had in mind before your mind became clouded with the judgments, criticisms, picture perfect posts, and opinions of others. Let's get you to that place by exploring and then simplifying the way you address tantrums.

Download the free Taming Tantrums workbook at wendybertagnole.com/workbook

Chapter One

THE ROLE OF THE PARENT

All behavior is a child's way of communicating an unmet need.
A parent's job is to decode that communication and, together with
the child, help address that need.

Let's talk about how that is going to happen. It all starts with changing the way we, as parents and caregivers address our children's needs when they begin to surface in the form of tantrums, meltdowns, or other challenging behavior. Throughout this book we will assume that "all behavior is simply a form of communication," a concept I wish I would have known during those tough years in early motherhood.

A New Perspective

I've heard it said that parenting is way of looking in the mirror at all the emotions we've ever had in our lives. When our kids do something amazing, wonderful, and awesome, our hearts fill to the brim with pride. When our child ends up being the bully on the playground, a deep sense of guilt and embarrassment overcomes us as we wonder where we went wrong in our parenting roles.

We tend to feel as though what our children do reflects on our parenting abilities. We see it that way because we are emotionally tied to our children's actions. For that reason, when we see anything other than what we define as "good behavior," we immediately jump in and try to fix the problem, because it seems like a slap in the face to our parenting skills. While we may FEEL that way, reality is very different from that.

Understanding this concept is what brought me out of my broken parenting role and into a place of my kids having fewer tantrums, more communication, and much more peace in our home. It didn't happen overnight, but it all started with a shift in the way I saw and internalized tantrums.

The Parenting Garden

If our parenting lives were compared to a garden, our children's challenging behaviors and tantrums would undoubtedly be the weeds-- those things we all hate, try to avoid, and want to get rid of as quickly as possible. As anyone who has ever had a garden will know, there are two natural ways of getting rid of weeds: cutting them down, or pulling them up by the roots. (Of course you can blast them with weed killer, but that doesn't seem appropriate when comparing it to kids, so I'll leave that one out).

Parents are like nurturers, like gardeners who plant seeds, spend hours watering, and then worry about the tiny little plants that will soon grow to their full potential. But, before the plants emerge, a few weeds pop up, destroying the perfect image of the gardener. The gardener becomes embarrassed of the weeds in the garden he worked so hard to grow. In frustration, he goes out and trims them all down to ground level, invisible to anyone who passes by. Although his garden looks perfect for the moment, in reality it is full of all the same weeds he began with, they are just below the surface. Every day he clips down any sight of the weeds and tells himself his garden looks perfect, just the way he always imagined. The price he pays for his perfect garden is that every day he has to chop weeds to maintain that look he strives for.

That's exactly what I was doing in the first few years of motherhood. I kept up a good façade on the outside, but under the surface we had massive meltdowns, yelling matches, and more tantrums than I would care to admit. We had a lot of weeds in our garden. I did a great job cutting those down so most people wouldn't see them.

This scenario is more common than we realize. While most of us are desperately trying to be "good parents" who "have it all together," reality is tantrums happen, challenging behaviors happen, and the way we address them matters. They're just like weeds, everyone has them.

Most of the time, when we see these behavior weeds pop up, we want an immediate solution to make it disappear. So we send our kid to timeout, have them put their nose to the wall, or scold them to show that we are "taking care of the situation."

Ironically, when asked about any of those parenting methods, the majority of parents say they don't work in the long run. The same behaviors keep happening no matter what the parent does, which makes parenting feel exhausting and frustrating.

The reason that happens is because those parenting methods are all forms of mowing down the weeds. It's a form of cutting the behavior off at the very end, to make it go away. None of these typical parenting methods (which I used tirelessly day in and day out) get the parent to the root of the behavior (we will discuss more of this in chapter 2). Unless you solve the root of the issue, those behaviors will surface again and again, forcing the parent to always be on guard, ready to discipline and maintain consistency. That stage is likely where you are stuck right now, most parents are. It's exhausting, it doesn't work in the long run, and there is a much more effective way.

Now let's imagine that when the gardener sees the weeds, instead of trying to hide them to protect his image as the "expert gardener," he does something different. This time, he acknowledges that his weed chopping efforts are not solving the problem, so he plans a chunk of time each day to pluck each of those weeds out by the root. It is more time consuming at first, but in the long run, this garden will need much less maintenance and will bring sweet tasting fruit. Sure, weeds will still pop up from time to time, but when they do, he will pluck those out just as easily as he did the others. It is part of the process of having a plentiful garden, and he is willing to put in the extra work to get to the root and solve the problem completely.

So it is with parenting. We have to take the time to get to the root of our children's negative behaviors and eventually most of them will disappear.

In workshops when I teach parents to start addressing behavior from the root, the changes that happen are incredible and almost immediate. Royalle, for example, a student who participated in the Raising Kids Who Listen[1] workshop, was having a hard time with her 7 year old daughter. When Royalle came to me she felt that her daughter was a good kid, but would only listen to her dad. If Royalle said anything, it either caused a fight, or her daughter would refuse to

[1] https://wendybertagnole.com/raising-kids-who-listen/

obey. The tension between the two of them was tangible and had been increasing for over a year. Royalle had tried being harsh, being patient, using timeouts, and everything else in the book. She was cutting down the weeds of her daughters behavior, and felt exhausted.

After just two days of addressing the root of this behavior, Royalle said "after school, we were bringing everything in from the car, which usually initiates the sassy attitude and refusal to do anything. Instead, I used your techniques and my daughter picked up my purse on her own and said 'I'll help you mommy.' I was surprised at how sweet she was and wanted to ask 'who are you and what did you do with my daughter?' It was a nice relief and the rest of our evening went well too. I can't believe how easy this is! I'm naturally more patient, and she is naturally less resistant to me."

From here on out, I invite you to take the perspective of the gardener who wants to get to the root of the weed problem. Doing so will feel different but trust me, once you see the power of this method, like Royalle did, you won't want to go back to just clipping the top of the weeds ever again.

This is where you go from being a parent who tries to control reactions (mowing down weeds), to being a parent who is proactively dealing with behaviors instead of trying to do damage control after they pop up. Remember, changing your response to negative behavior is a process, not an immediate solution. It won't work perfectly every time, but by just trying you are miles ahead of where you started!

In the next chapter you will learn about the different layers of your children's behavior and how to start responding more effectively by exposing the root of it all.

Put It Into Practice:

Write down some examples of how you have been influenced by others' parenting advice and ignored your own instincts. Reflect on those and how you can begin to change your mindset to better deal with those situations.

Chapter Two

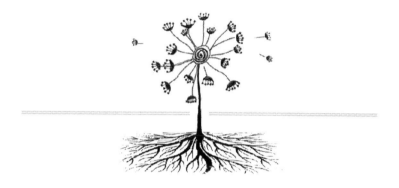

UNDERSTANDING DIFFICULT BEHAVIOR

The Weed Analogy

*I*n the last chapter we talked about behavior being similar to a weed that will continue to grow back until its root is plucked. Now we are going to take the time to really understand what that root is and eventually how to get to it so we can start addressing the problem more effectively. This is the Behavior Weed method.

Exposing the Root of Behavior

One evening last year, after making a quick dinner for the kids, rushing through homework, just in time to dig through mounds of laundry to find my sons baseball uniform, I asked him to get ready so we could get out the door on time. We were rushed, and of course he was literally dragging his feet, whining, and complaining about going. With each complaint he mumbled my frustration began to rise. I could feel myself at the brink of exploding. After all I had done to get everything ready, I did NOT appreciate his laziness and lack of concern about going to practice. For a moment I thought "how am I raising such a lazy and unmotivated child? What did I do wrong?" Then, before I could act on that thought, it happened.

With tears in his eyes and arms crossed over his chest he let it all out; "I hate baseball, I DON'T want to go, and you can't make me. You're the one who signed me up, I didn't even want to do it. You CAN'T make me go!"

It felt like suddenly my parenting garden was flooded with weeds.

My initial "mom reaction" was to yell right back. I had to counteract his stubbornness. I had to show him whose boss and tell him to stop whining, suck it up, and stick to the sport he had chosen (yes, he had in fact chosen baseball, but in this moment of frustration he was blaming me for it). I had a full speech in my head about how we aren't quitters and why it's not good to give up, just like any mom would do, but I resisted my urge to mow the weeds down. Lecturing and then forcing him to go would have been addressing the top of the weed, and always ends up in a power struggle. He would likely end up in more tears, I would feel awful, and baseball practice wouldn't even be an option for the evening.

Because I'd been practicing the behavior weed method, I knew this behavior was coming from a root, much deeper than I was seeing on the surface. It still took everything I had in me to push aside my knee jerk reaction and engage in a series of questions, gently guiding him towards the real problem, or the root.

Instead of enforcing strict rules and guidelines as a response to his resistance, I kept repeating things like "ok, that's fine, can you tell me why?" or "I hear you don't want to go, that's ok, let's talk about that." After about a minute of this gentle guidance he exposed the root on his own and said "I just don't like going because last time at practice I lost you and I got scared. I don't want to lose you again!"

He was having a tantrum because he was AFRAID, not because he was being defiant, lazy, or uncooperative. The root was a real feeling he had to overcome. Had I jumped in with my lecture, I would have completely missed the mark. I would not have seen the true root of his behavior, and because of that, my solution wouldn't have done anything to help him. The tantrum would have gone on, and I would have felt out of control, and likely would have ended up punishing him.

Sound familiar? We all do it. That's what we've been trained to do! Let's dig a little deeper to see why this scenario happens, over and over again.

The Behavior Weed Process Explained

The first step to getting to the root of any behavior is looking at it from a different angle. Typically, when we see our children doing something "naughty" we assume they are making a willful choice. We then interpret that choice as a reflection on the child's personality (my child is just stubborn, manipulative, emotional, whiney, defiant, etc.), or as a direct reflection of our own inadequate parenting (I'm not strict enough, I'm not consistent enough, I don't have the energy to keep up, etc.). Those thoughts cause us, as parents, to want to immediately stop the child's challenging behavior because we think it reflects poorly on us and on our kids.

While it is tempting to think that a rotten personality, a difficult phase, or a horrible parenting style is at the root of a particular behavior, most often it is something deeper, just like the case with my son going to baseball practice. Unfortunately, the typical parenting strategies—time outs, grounding, scolding, spanking, lecturing, putting soap in the mouth, etc.-- don't help us dig deeper into the true causes of behavior. Every single one of those is designed to discourage the child from engaging in that behavior. When we only focus on the top of the weed, we see it coming back again and again. That's why the child who goes to timeout today will go there tomorrow and the next day and the next until she learns to be more sneaky or until you, as the parent, give up that particular fight. That isn't sustainable, it's frustrating. I don't know about you, but I don't have time or energy for that!

A Better Solution

After studying children's most challenging and extreme behavior for many years, clinical psychologist Ross Greene discovered a groundbreaking concept that addresses this problem, which affects our whole society. He realized that as parents we tend to look at our children's behavior with the idea that kids do well when they <u>want</u> to. We punish, discipline, etc., so they won't want to engage in that behavior anymore. We rationalize that kids will <u>want</u> to "be good" in order to avoid our punishments. That might work on very passive kids, but for most others (the ones we are raising), it ends up causing arguments, fights, and power struggles that simply make parenting miserable, and do very little to change the behavior. Thankfully, Ross Greene suggests that a more powerful way to approach this is with the idea that "kids do well when they <u>can</u>."

Behavior Is Communication

The most effective way to address challenging behavior is to help the child solve the root that is actually causing the behavior, so they are <u>capable</u> of doing well. As in the example of my son not wanting to go to baseball practice, I needed to address the fear that caused the behavior, because without doing that the behavior would have continued.

When behavior is seen as a child's call for help, rather than a sign of willful stubbornness or defiance, a parent can then help the child figure out how to deal with the issue at hand. The behavior acts as a clue for parents, to help uncover the root of the problem behind it.

If we take a minute to think about it, we realize that "behavior" is the way humans have always communicated that something is wrong. Babies cry when they are hungry, uncomfortable, scared, or in pain. Crying is the first form of communication humans have, and it is a very powerful way of expressing feelings before verbal language is learned. Even after a child acquires language he will still use behavior to express feelings that are difficult to communicate with words. Feelings and emotions, are difficult to express or admit. Even adults have a hard time being vulnerable enough to say "I'm really nervous about things, which is causing me to be less patient today." So most often, when our child is hurt, feels uncomfortable, is disappointed etc., parents see the behavior, because it's the easiest way to say "something is off."

For example, when my 6 year old felt scared about being left at baseball, he expressed that through crying and whining. He didn't have the words or emotional intelligence to tell me "mom I'm scared you'll leave me", so they came out as behavior.

Interpreting the behavior through the lens of helping a child so they <u>can</u> do well, is the system I will outline in this book: First, see the behavior; then, identify the root; and finally guide the child through the process of solving the issue causing the weed together with you.

The Meaning Behind the Behavior

That day, before baseball practice, I saw my son's tantrum was rooted in his fear. I took a minute to tell him how I would be by his side and in his sight during this practice, and asked if that would help. He said yes, and two minutes later he was happy as could be and excited for practice. His rant about quitting had nothing to do with any of the bullet points in the speech I was about to give him. It had everything to do with an underlying fear he had about something that had happened the previous week, something I didn't realize at the time would have such a powerful effect.

This is just one of many experiences with my children that have taught me their challenging behavior is not just a discipline problem needing a quick punishment, it is an opportunity to understand their emotions, and to guide them toward ways to solve similar problems that might arise in the future. Had I followed through with my initial reaction, I would have forced him into compliance but I never would have discovered he was afraid of losing me.

Where Typical Parenting Strategies Fall Short

If what most parents say is true, that typical parenting strategies like timeouts, yelling, being more consistent, don't really work. Why do we use them? Why do we hold on to the idea that we "should" be doing these?

Behaviorists subscribe to the idea that our behavior has a purpose, and when a behavior is successful in meeting a need, it will happen more often. That idea leads to the conclusion that if a behavior doesn't meet a need, it happens less often.

Four main "needs" have emerged from this research, which many parents now use as guidelines for understanding behavior. Those four reasons include:

- To attract attention
- To **escape** a situation, an event, or a person
- To **gain access** to something they want
- To react to a **sensory** response

With that approach in mind, it's easy for a well-meaning parent to say "if a kid is whining to get your attention, just ignore him and the whining will go away. He will learn that if he wants your attention, he will only get it when he doesn't whine."

Or, "If my kid is gagging on her food and crying about eating it, clearly she is just trying to get out of (or escape) dinner and will go directly for the dessert. So, I need to be bigger than her, stay consistent and eventually she will 'grow out of' her picky eating habits."

While those might sound like they are counteracting the "needs for behavior," new research shows us, there's more to it than that.

Parents assume that there is a "payoff" somewhere. The behavior is being reinforced. It "works" somehow to meet a need, and if it doesn't "work" it will stop.

A friend of mine, and behaviorist, said this about assuming behavior has a "payoff". "This is where I went wrong as a mother. My son kept running into the same brick wall over and over again, because of the "lagging skills" Dr. Greene describes. I was emotionally disconnected when he misbehaved (this worked really well when I was a therapist, not so much as a parent) but I thought that if I stayed calm, the natural consequences would help him learn. Not so much."

Dr. Greene's approach helps parents to assess the real reason for behavior in a deeper and more meaningful way, so that families can discover the root of challenging behavior instead of focusing on how to control the resulting disruptions.

Ross Greene challenged the popular assumption that "kids do well when they wanna." He asserted that "kids do well when they CAN." After conducting extensive research, he concluded that although behavior CAN be purely willful, most often there is a deeper root causing it. He suggests that the reason for most children's behavior is that they lack the necessary skills to solve the problems in daily life. Using Greene's research and my own experiences with sensory processing, I've come up with a model I call the "behavior weed," which combines both these theories into a visual image that is easy to remember.

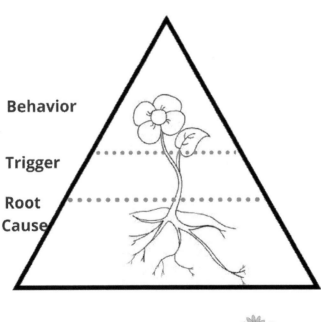

The flower at the top of the weed is the negative behavior. It's what most people see and what most parents react to. It's the hitting, crying, whining, defiance, etc.

The stem represents the trigger, which would be the action or event that seems to provoke the behavior. The stem could consist of such things as:

- being told "no" (which would result in a tantrum which could be perceived as form of trying to gain attention)
- delaying sleep at bedtime (which could be seen as trying to get access to something)
- a child refusing a particular food (which could be seen as an escape mechanism)

For my son the stem was the process of getting ready for t-ball practice. Parents who've been taught the applied behaviorist theories might run through the list of four functions and chalk the behavior up to just a call for attention or a way of escaping an undesirable activity, then responding accordingly. I could have said to myself "my son just wants to get out of going to practice, he is clearly doing this to escape his responsibility of showing up to baseball." But, as we saw, that wasn't the true root of his behavior, it was simply the trigger.

What I'm suggesting in this book is that you lay aside the typical parenting theories of behavior (seeking escape, gaining access, or attracting attention) and focus instead on digging a little deeper to expose the true root in the situation by simply asking "why?". Why is the child wanting attention? Why is the child trying to escape, and why is the child trying to gain access to something? By asking these questions we get closer to the root issue. From here on out we will focus on not just chopping down the stem in hopes that the weed will go away for good. We have to keep digging.

To uncover the root, we need to dig deeper to find the meaning being communicated by the behavior. Typically, the roots consist of:

- the need for power
- the need for predictability
- skills that are lacking (including expressing emotions)
- the need to regulate the sensory system.

Parents who have tried my "weed approach" find themselves engaged in fewer power struggles, facing less defiance and fewer meltdowns, not because they have mastered the right strategies to address the extreme reactions, but because they have supported their children in a process of being less reactive in the first place. Fewer initial reactions lead to fewer challenging behaviors and more happy times for your family!

<u>Put It Into Practice</u>

1. Write down a list of triggers that commonly spark behavioral issues in your child.

2. Compose a list of triggers that cause you, as a parent, to react in negative ways.

Chapter Three

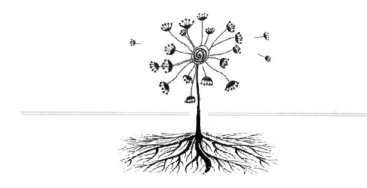

ADDRESSING BEHAVIOR

An Introduction to the PULLS System

"How do I stop a tantrum?"

"What do I do when my kid freaks out?"

"How can I help my child who withdraws?"

"What do I do about my picky eater who won't try anything?"

I can't tell you the number of emails, messages, and phone calls I receive from parents asking those exact questions. The answer doesn't lie in some quick fix or 10- day challenge. Instead it comes from exposing that root we have talked so much about.

We've discussed why behavior happens and our role as parents in digging deeper to expose the root. Now, let's get into specific strategies of addressing the roots of behavior.

Effectively Addressing Behavior

The other day my 6-year-old threw a fit in the middle of church. He couldn't handle the fact that his marker box had two fewer markers than his sister's. The thought of her having more than he did set off some intense (and loud) emotional reactions. The old me wanted to say "seriously, they are markers, get over it kid!" But time has shown me that approach doesn't work. So, I picked him up and headed to a more private space where we could deal with the issue. With tears in his eyes and his face red with frustration, he wrapped his arms and legs tightly around me as I carried him out of the chapel.

As I left, I saw and felt the eyes of friends and neighbors on me. Most of those people probably figured I was headed out with the intention of putting my son in timeout, punishing him, or reprimanding him for being noisy and irrational. Doing so MIGHT have taught him not to have emotional outbursts in public, but it would not have taught him how to actually work through the frustrations at the root of his little freak-out session.

Before I tell you the rest of the story, let's look at the layers of behavior in this situation. The top of the weed was my son screaming and crying, the most visible part of the entire situation. The trigger was the intensity of his emotions about his sister's marker box having more markers in it than his did. What was the root of it all that made him so sensitive to the number of markers his sister had?

If we go back to the 4 roots of behavior we see they are;

- the need for power
- the need for predictability

- lacking skills to deal with a problem
- the inability to regulate sensory needs.

In this situation, I believe the root was <u>lacking the skill</u> of being able to deal with the disappointment of having fewer markers and effectively find a solution to his problem.

To help him learn that skill and eventually solve his own problem, I went through a few steps I've developed, called the PULLS method, that help get me to the true root of most of my children's behavioral issues. I outline my exact process in more detail on the next page

So, as we walked into an empty room, I put him down and he let his feelings all out. He started yelling, crying, and screaming about all the things he felt were unfair. He screamed and cried and said he wanted to take the markers away from his sister, reasoning that if he couldn't have all the markers, she couldn't either. I listened, told him it was ok to feel mad, reminded him it would be disrespectful to take his sister's markers away, bit my tongue to keep from freaking out at him, then focused again on just listening.

When he yelled things that were absurd, I gently stated a boundary to let him know he wasn't going to get whatever he wanted, and that he needed to solve his own problem. It took a while, but he calmed down enough to work through a solution with me as I gave him the space and power to do so. He finally decided he would ask his sister to let him borrow a marker so that they would both have an equal number of markers, then when they returned home they would look for the missing markers together.

Was it perfect? No! Was there a tantrum? Yes! But was he able to solve the problem on his own in the end? YES! He did it all on his own. I was there to support him, guide him, and draw clear boundaries when needed. He did it using the same process he will have available to him for the rest of his life whenever something upsets him, so taking the time to walk him through it while he is young is important to me.

Now let's look more specifically at each step in the parent's process of uncovering the root reasons for a child's behavior and then doing something about it.

The steps are what I like to call PULLS:

- Power share
- Understand your child's feelings/roots of the problem
- Lower walls by supporting sensory
- Live together, laugh often
- Solve problems together

In the next five chapters we will walk through each of these steps, outlining what each step of this PULLS process looks like, why it is important, and how to use it effectively.

Put It Into Practice:

Make a copy of the PULLS method to getting to the root of the behavioral weed. Keep it in plain sight to remind yourself where to focus when emotions rise and all eyes are on you to make it stop.

Chapter Four

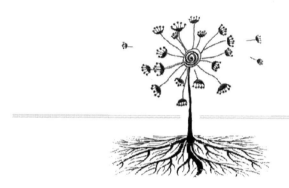

Power Share

In 2016 I sent a survey to over 7,000 parents asking what the most common problem was in their home. It came as no surprise that most parents responded that they felt their kids did not listen to them, respect them, or even care what they said. They felt they had NO power as parents.

For parents, that feels threatening. It feels awful. I get it. I used to feel so enraged when my three-year-old would stand with her shoulders squared, arms crossed, while looking me in the eye and saying "no, I won't!" I never would have DARED do that as a child, so having my child do that to me sent me into a fury of striving for power.

A friend of mine was going through a similar situation in her home more recently and posted about it on Facebook. I was amazed as I scrolled through all the mom advice offered to her. Among the dozens of comments, I saw things like:

"Just be stronger than her, she will eventually give in."

"Stand your ground, if you give in once she will take advantage of you."

"Stay consistent, that's what works for me."

My heart ached as I read the comments I knew would only take my friend deeper into the struggle she was already in. I remembered the time I was so deeply entrenched in dishing out all the punishments, being firm, staying consistent, and doing everything that was recommended. All of that just made things worse inside my own home, which made me feel like a failure for not being able to make it work in my home.

Sadly, my home wasn't the only one caught in this vicious cycle where everyone is fighting to be the boss, but in the end, nobody really wins. The solution to this problem is to simply share the power.

On Obeying and Listening

This was true for Lindsey, a student in my Comprehensive Online Behavior program. She felt like her daughter was very defiant, stubborn, and strong willed. Getting her to do the most simple thing like making her bed, turned into a meltdown, or a massive argument most every day. Lindsey hated fighting with her 4 year old, but still wanted to teach her how to be respectful and keep the home clean, so she persisted. She didn't back down, but inside she wondered why couldn't her daughter just listen and obey one simple rule? She felt torn by how to make that happen.

After practicing this concept of sharing the power, Lindsey found her daughter to be "naturally willing to help." Some days her daughter would remind herself that her bed needed to be made, and talked openly about the importance of it. The fights didn't happen as often, and the relationship between Lindsey and her daughter improved more than either of them could have ever imagined.

As parents we are taught that we are the bosses, we make the decisions, and those decisions should be respected by our children. That respect comes in the form of compliance to the decisions we make and the rules we set. But as the parenting survey (and my own personal experience) revealed, most parents find that this approach causes more problems than not.

Why Share Power?

While most parents feel it is important to share power on less important tasks like which socks to wear, or if they want to eat peas or carrots with their dinner, not every choice is that simple. Problems surface and kids dig in their heels when there's a rule to be followed, a chore to do, or something you just need your child to listen to. When a kid starts resisting, typically that's a cue for parents to counteract the resistance with more resistance, until someone gives in. It's a constant battle to see who can hold the power, one I know all too well.

My oldest tends to be the most affected when he doesn't have enough power given to him. We had our times of battling for power over even the smallest of things. I remember at its worst, we fought mostly over the amount of time he spent on the iPad. I'd ask him to get off, he'd ignore me. I'd tell him to get off, and he'd respond sternly with a "No! I'm not going to get off, I'm in the middle of something."

That was always the beginning of our fights where I'd threaten to take his iPad away, or I'd ground him from it, or do whatever I could to feel like I was standing in my rightful parental power.

No matter what I did, we still fought weekly. Until I learned that I didn't have to have sole ownership over the power in our home. He could have power as well. I changed my approach, still kept my expectations, and together we still work through his allotment of iPad time. We do so now with much fewer fights.

When we have a rule and we tell a child directly to obey it without question, he feels powerless because we are hoarding the power. When a person's power is taken from them, the natural reaction is to react by immediately putting up an emotional wall of defense. The parent then feels the resistance and has to fight harder to power through that wall, and the child reacts by sending more reinforcements. It's a constant battle to see who can be more powerful; the parent who set the rule or the child who defies the rule, both are exerting their power to control another person. We've all been there. It's an uphill battle without a winner in the end. So where does the power of the parent and the power for the child all come together to make peace while still maintaining parental boundaries?

The Process

To show you how sharing power happens, Cynthia Tobias, author of the book *You Can't Make Me But I Can Be Persuaded*, uses an analogy I find helpful. She suggests parents should have the power to decide "where to go" and allow the child to have the power to decide "how to get there." Essentially, parents should state their boundary or expectation and then let the child decide what the process of making that happen will look like. In this way, everyone shares the power, which is exactly what Lindsey did so successfully with her very strong-willed daughter.

The best way a parent can allow that to happen is to make fewer demands and ask more questions. The main reason this strategy is effective is that when demands are made a child has two choices: submit and obey, OR defy and deny. The first leaves the child feeling powerless. The second leaves her feeling powerful. For a person seeking power, the second choice will be the most common response. On the other hand, the child who always submits might seem like the perfect child, but that child is not learning valuable skills of making decisions and taking responsibility for them. Neither scenario is productive in the long run. Because our goal as parents is to support our children and help them learn how to solve their own problems, I suggest avoiding demands and statements as much as possible.

Turning Demands into Questions to Share Power

Asking the child questions is an important way to share power, but has to be done in the right way. The guidelines I like to use when asking questions are summarized here:

- Avoid questions that require only a "yes or no" response (unless the child is nonverbal or has limited vocabulary). For example, rather than asking "Do you want to eat broccoli for dinner?" (because the answer will likely be "no"), instead try "which vegetable would you like to eat tonight?"

- Avoid giving limited options, go for open ended options instead. Allow the child to come up with the options as often as possible (unless the child is nonverbal or has limited vocabulary). For example, rather than asking "Would you like to wear the blue shirt or the red one today?" (which can make a child feel powerless with the limited choices given), instead try "We just put away all your laundry, which outfit would you like to wear tomorrow?"

- After stating your boundary, ask a question that gives the child the power to determine the process of the situation. For example, rather than demanding "Get off your iPad or you won't have any friend time or dessert for the week," try instead, "As soon as you are off your iPad, I we can talk about what to do when your friend comes over. What would you like to have for snack when that happens?"

Notice that my advice is different if you are dealing with a child who has a limited or no verbal skills. Children who don't have the words to express what they want need simpler questions given to them, so "yes" or "no" questions are appropriate ways to guide them toward solving their own problems. A parent might say, for instance, "It looks like you are upset. I noticed you are covering your ears. Is a sound bothering you?" or "I see you came to your room to cry. I'm here to help you get through this if you'd like. Do you need more alone time?" By stating your observations of their behavior and asking for validation, you can absolutely guide children with limited or no vocabulary through this same supportive process.

For all other children, asking questions within the guidelines above is a great way to give them the power to make decisions and solve his own problems, with you as a guide.

When a Child Won't Cooperate

When Lindsey first started the program, she and her daughter were engaging in daily power struggles. As life has it, when we try to learn a new skill, we usually end up falling down a few times before we get it right. One night I received an emotional message from Lindsey after trying to share power, but seeing the same result as before. Her daughter was in tears, Lindsey had emotionally checked out and told husband to take over while she calmed down and talked through it with me.

Lindsey's family (her husband and two kids, both under 4 years old) were on a vacation for a few days. She decided that to save a little money, they would buy cereal to eat each morning they were in the hotel. To make it a little more fun, and to give her daughter some power, she took her daughter to the cereal aisle and said "I know we don't usually eat cereal at home, but since this is a vacation and we want it to be fun, we are going to let you choose the cereal for the week. Which one would you like?"

Lindsey felt good about sharing power, and her daughter felt excited to have so many choices of food she didn't usually get to have. So, as a four-year-old would, she picked out the cereal WITH marshmallows AND sprinkles in it, which meant sugar overload. Clearly, not what Lindsey had in mind.

At the thought of her kids starting the day on a sugar high while on vacation, Linsey put her foot down and said "that one looks like there's too much sugar in it, is there one with less sugar, like maybe this same one without the marshmallows, that we can get?"

Her daughter said "No, I want this one, you said I could pick it out, and I want this one."

That was the beginning of a 30-minute crying session and a mad dash out of the grocery store without the box of cereal her daughter had chosen.

Sometimes, as in Lindsey's case, this process won't go perfectly, and when that happens I want you to have a backup plan. I use one of two options as a backup plan.

First, in Lindsey's situation, she failed to set boundaries before asking the open-ended question. Going back on her word really frustrated her child, so she could have counted that one as a lesson learned for HER to be more specific and anticipate boundaries before handing over the power.

In this scenario, I would have advised Lindsey to tell her daughter that one looked like a lot of sugar and ask if there was another cereal she would like instead. If her daughter were to say no, I'd advise her to go with that choice and remember in the future to state that boundary first. We always learn from our mistakes.

The second scenario is one I would use if a child refuses to answer the question. When that happens, we typically want to jump in and threaten, punish, or force kids to answer, reality is that doing so wouldn't solve anything. The most productive solution is to state your observation or boundary, let the child know where you stand and where her limitations are, and move on. For example:

- If you've asked your child which dishes she will do, and she ignores that question. Try placing a positive thing after what it is you're asking. For example "You can get on your iPad after the dishes are done. Which dishes will you be doing today?"
- If you've told your son he has 10 more minutes to play and he says "no," give him a bit of space then reframe; "Our time at the park is up in 5 minutes. What would you like to do for your last activity?"
- If you know your child refuses most everything you make for dinner, try saying; "I'm making a menu for the week. Which three dinners would you like me to add to it?"
- If you try to talk but your kid gives you "the look", try this; "It seems like you are really mad. What happened?"
- If your kid is quiet and not talking about a situation, try stating it this way; "I saw you were playing with Joe and then hit him. I can tell you are really upset. What's going on?"

Questions are a powerful way to place the responsibility in the hands of children to solve their own problems with you by their side. Essentially, everyone shares the power, and is happier, and less defensive because of it.

Put It Into Practice:

1. Write down common statements you find yourself saying to your child and then turn them into questions to share the power with your child.

Chapter Five

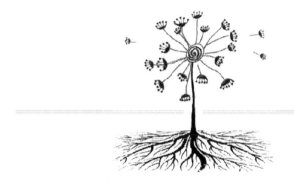

PROVIDE **U**NDERSTANDING

*A*t my house I used to dread every single school day. Every morning I would try my best to do everything perfectly; wake them up at a decent time, have breakfast ready for them, have clothes laid out for them, and lunches all made. I worked tirelessly to make sure their mornings were as easy as possible. No matter what I tried, most mornings still ended in massive meltdowns before school. There would be tears, questions, whining, refusing to get ready, you name it, my kids did it. If we look back at the typical behaviorist parenting style, most people would say that the reason for this is a ploy for children who want to escape responsibilities of getting ready in the morning and going to school. While that is partially true, as always, there's a deeper root to that behavior, which is what I found to be the case in my own home.

In the midst of these morning meltdown years I read an interesting insight in a book, one that will stick with me forever. It said the world of children is very unpredictable because they don't know what's on the agenda every day like an adult does. Kids don't have a concept of time, and therefore they tend to live in the moment. They don't think about the future like adults do. I'm pretty sure that as an adult I'm ALWAYS living in the future, as I clearly showed when I was frantically trying each morning to prepare everything for my kids before they woke up to try and avoid any meltdowns.

Kids live almost completely in the moment because they aren't aware of things that can or will happen in the future. They don't know what to expect, and for many kids, the unknown is scary. Because the unknown is scary when they are face to face with it, they resist it, they fight it, and they don't want to face it. The result? Tantrums!

Remember when I told you about the 4 true roots of behavior in Chapter 2? One of those is the need for a greater understanding of the future, or predictability. The lack of predictability causes so many meltdowns, tantrums, power struggles, and other difficult behaviors in our children, because it is scary to them.

The antidote to that situation is easier than most parents think. Before learning of this concept, my approach to these morning meltdowns was very traditional: dish out the punishments. "If you don't get ready on time you won't get any electronics time after school." Or "Do this now or I'll take away your iPad for a week." Whatever form it might take, the natural parental reaction is to punish, because that's what we are taught to do.

I punished and punished, but nothing changed except the tension in our home. As it grew stronger as I began to dread each morning. I didn't like being mean first thing in the morning. I hated the fights. Essentially, I was fighting a losing battle, and completely missing the true root of the tantrums; the need for predictability.

Things Started to Change

When I added an extra couple of minutes to our evening routines to provide my kids with a better understanding about the plans for the next day, things changed. Each night as I tucked them into bed, we would run through the next day's agenda and encourage a discussion about it. Every morning when they woke up, I'd remind them of the plans, and add anything else I could think of to help them truly understand and get a feeling for what the day would look like.

The future isn't as scary when it isn't a mystery.

As the morning meltdowns began to fade (we still see them every now and then), I realized I could apply the same concept to so many other parts of our day. Going to the grocery store, running errands, going to a friend's house, any event that happened in the day, my kids handled it better when they knew exactly what to expect.

Most of the time this is as easy as talking about an event before it happens.

After doing a 1:1 consultation with friend of mine, she saw the same success in her home almost immediately. She came to me one day telling me that she couldn't go anywhere with her kids. Any time they went to the park, a friend's, house, a birthday party, or anywhere outside of their home, her kids all clung to her and started whining.

She tried everything to get them to just play like all the rest of the kids around them. My friend admitted that most nights she would go to bed frustrated and in tears, wondering what she had done to create such needy kids. She admitted she felt like a failure and was a little resentful towards her kids because they made social situations miserable.

After implementing a little more understanding and predictability into their day, the kids immediately responded. They planned to go to a friend's house the day after our consult, my friend took the time to talk to the kids about it, running through situations that might arise and asking the kids what they could do in those situations. An extra 20 minutes of prep time with her kids ended up creating a really fun and relaxing play date. The other mom, who had seen the kids acting whiney every time before this play date, was amazed at what a drastic difference was made in such short time.

This is proof of Ross Greene's theory that "kids do well when they can."

Taking a few minutes before going to the grocery store, play date, or even getting ready for school to talk about your expectations, what will and won't be allowed, and any potential problems that might occur can be that small change that creates a drastic difference. It could also include an extra minute or two during the bedtime routine to talk about the events planned for the next day. Students in my program report that if they just take a few minutes to look back at the list of the most tantrum filled times of the day, and think about ways to talk about those situations before they happen, tantrums dramatically decrease easily.

Some key things to remember when talking to your child about future things that might be scary:

- Visual schedules or reminders can help prepare a child for potentially frightening but necessary events (nail clipping day, dentist appointment, hair cut day, etc.)

- Empathize with your children and acknowledge their feelings when those fears surface
- Ask open ended-questions to dig deeper into possible problems (ex. We are going to a birthday party tomorrow. How do you feel about that? What don't you like about the last one you went to? What can we do to help you feel more comfortable?)
- Setting a specific day or week or month for routines that are particularly difficult can eliminate a lot of stress (shower day, nail clipping day, hair cut day, etc.)

Rules and Expectations

People thrive when they know what to expect. When it comes to setting rules, expectations, and boundaries, I encourage parents to create ones that are predictable and easy to remember, so kids have a solid understanding of them. The boundaries in your home will likely be different from those in my home. No matter what they are, they need to be simple, direct, and applicable to both the adults and children in your household.

One of the most important boundaries in our home is "respect other's bodies, requests, feelings, and space." We also have boundaries that pertain to safety issues, obedience to the law, and any rules that are asked of us in various places we go (in the library we whisper, at grandma's house we don't jump on couches, at school we don't hug other people, etc.).

My kids know the family boundaries and can repeat them. Any time I step into a situation, I draw upon our family boundaries to remind the kids of the expectations we have for every person in our home. That is not to say that I lecture them. Reminding my kids of the boundaries is a simple and direct process. Let's say, for example, that my daughter gets really mad and hits someone. Because she has crossed a line, I intervene. While validating her emotions (because I need to understand what is going on in that inner core), I say, "We respect other people's bodies in this house. Hitting is not respectful. I see that you are mad so I'm taking you to my room so our bodies can calm down and we are ready to be respectful."

I state the boundaries, without any blame or shame, and always in reference to what I have already established as rules in my own home. This serves to remind a child of where she crossed the line or is about to. It is a reminder, not a reprimand. Not a punishment.

For the most part, boundaries are most effectively communicated before explosive behavior happens. So when a child is sitting in the car seat and hasn't buckled her seatbelt, we say, "The car will leave when everyone is buckled. The law says we all have to buckle before we move." Or, when my kid asks if he can ride his bike, I respond by saying "Yes, we can have bike-riding time. As soon as I see helmets on all heads, we can start. The law says we all have to wear helmets." The key to setting any boundary is to be direct, keep it simple, and as often as possible avoid the word "you". For many reasons, hearing the word "you" can feel like finger pointing, and will often trigger an emotional wall (more about this in chapter 6).

After applying a little understanding to the more stressful, tantrum-filled parts of our day, I was relieved to see the positive change it had on our family. While we are far from tantrum-free or perfect, I can say our home is far less chaotic and frazzled. The other day I was getting my kids ready for an afternoon outing. I had provided an understanding of where we were going to go and what we were going to do, but my son wasn't having it. Because we are in the practice of talking about things before they happen, and sharing the power, my seven-year-old came up to me and said "Mom, I don't think it's a good idea to go to that restaurant. I don't like it, and my sister doesn't like it, but we all like the noodle place. Can't we just go there instead?"

Had I waited until we arrived to tell my kids the plans, the tantrum would have happened in the car right outside the restaurant, or even worse, inside the restaurant as I'm trying to order, which is never a fun way to start a meal in public. These days I'm not looking for perfection, just fewer meltdowns and more communication. Providing understanding gives us the time and space to do that.

<u>Put It Into Practice</u>

1. Look back at the common triggers you listed in chapter two and brainstorm a few ways to provide more understanding to each situation.

2. Write down the rules and expectations in your home, making them as concise and clear as possible. Them imagine some scenarios where you might defuse situations in which your child has breached these rules or expectations.

Chapter Six

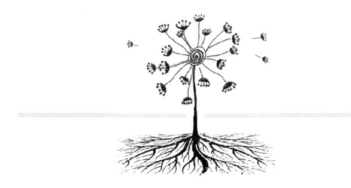

LOWER THE WALLS

The other day my son and I ran into something I like to call "the wall," or the emotional wall as I have alluded to in previous chapters. The long rainy season in our town had passed, the sky was bright blue, and there were no clouds to be seen. Being a person who loves to feel the warm rays of sun on my skin, and having kids who crave lots of physical movement, I decided we were going to spend the afternoon outside, which seemed like a perfect plan that would be met with no resistance at all.

Thrilled about my genius idea, I happily shared my plans with them, "Hey guys, the sun is out. Let's go find things to do outside." Being sure to avoid asking a yes/no question, giving them power to decide what exactly they would do, but still setting my expectation of where I wanted to be, I was feeling confident about the start of our day.

Two of my kids shared in my excitement, but the other crossed his arms over his chest, furrowed his brows, glared at me and said "Nope, I'm not going out there! You can't make me. It's stupid, it's dumb, and I DON'T want to go!"

As a child, I would NEVER have dared say those words to my parents. If I had, it would have resulted in a smack on the bum and some serious alone time in my room. I was raised to believe saying "no" was an act of defiance that was absolutely not tolerated because it diminished the power and authority of the parent. We now know, power can be shared, but hearing the word "No" so strongly still causes a knee jerk reaction in my heart, making me want to stand my ground, show them whose boss, and not ever be undermined again. By now, I know better than to act on that reaction because, it never works.

The Great Wall of Resistance

As I mentioned before, the wall is a defensive mechanism most humans develop to protect themselves. We put it up when we feel threatened, unsafe, or unsure in any way. It is part of the "fight, flight, or freeze" response we are all born with, and is perfectly natural.

As parents, we tend to throw that wall up when our power or authority feels threatened. A 3-foot-tall human holding his or her ground can feel threatening, so we put up a wall and fight to stand our ground.

In *The Conscious Parent,* Shefali Tsabary states, "Generations the world over have subscribed to an approach to parenting which states that, by reason of age and experience, the parent is at the top of a pyramid and the child by default at the bottom. The idea is that children should fit into the parent's world, not the other way around." So with this idea parents "tend to become hooked on control. If anything goes wrong or we are pushed just a little too far, we lose our balance" and punish, yell, engage in power plays, and anything else we can do to regain our footing.

For kids, that wall goes up when they feel pressured to do something outside their comfort zone, when their power feels threatened (which is why we share power), or when they are unsure of something (which is why we provide understanding). In those instances, their usual reaction is the stance my son took: furrowed brow, arms crossed, and feet firmly planted to stand their ground. Does that response sound familiar to you my friend? Likely that's why you are reading this book. Don't worry, by the end of this chapter you'll see solid ways to avoid that wall.

The Unseen Attack

Given their unpredictable and no-power world, children often resort to wall-building, but there's often a subtler reason it happens, one most parents might not realize. It has to do with the sensory system. We all have one, most of us don't understand the power of the body's senses.

Any child whose sensory system is out of balance will use this wall even more often than most kids. The child's body might resist things like certain textures of food, the smell of cooking, the feeling of rough clothing on the body, or the piercing feeling on the skin from each drop of water from a shower, among many other things. When this happens, the body puts up a wall in an effort to protect itself. Often it is easy to label a child defiant, manipulative, overly sensitive, or bullheaded, when in fact she is simply exhibiting a natural response to a sensory aversion.

For more information on the complete sensory system, what it looks like and how it may be affecting your child's behavior, download the free workbook at www.wendybertagnole.com.

Lowering the Wall

When parents and children both approach each other with walls up, a power struggle ignites and someone ends up on the losing end. It's easy to do because we've been taught to be bigger, stronger, and more stubborn than our kids. The only way to avoid the power struggle is to take both those walls down. That can only happen by using one important tool.

On that gorgeously sunny day when I stood face to face with my child who was absolutely determined NOT to do what I had asked, I put my own wall down. I lowered my defenses and leveled the playing field. There was no use pushing. He had something to say, but didn't have the words to say it, so we had to lower his wall.

I said, "What's up bud? I can see you don't want to go outside."

No threats, no reprimands for "defiance." There was no need. This wasn't a game to see who could be bigger, stronger, or more threatening. This was an opportunity to get to the true root of his behavior and hear what was going on inside of him.

"I don't know where my shoes are, and I don't like my sandals because every time I wear them I trip and I don't like it. So, NO I'm not going outside. I'm not going anywhere!"

He had a very real concern and couldn't find a solution on his own. The root of his behavior came from a skill he was lacking: his inability to communicate his needs or find an alternate solution to his problem (a pattern we see often in his life).

The tool I used to turn it all around was empathy. Empathy bridged that gap between him and me, lowered my wall, and allowed his wall to be lowered too.

When a child's wall goes up, no one other than the child can take it down. The more a parent pushes against it, the more reinforcements a child places behind it and the quicker it comes up in the future. The only way to get the wall down is to show children that you are on their side, so they feel safe. They need to know that you aren't going to push, force, bribe, or coerce them into anything. Once you've truly stepped into the role of supporter, that wall will go down, and empathy is the first step toward allowing that to happen.

Empathy allows us the opportunity to validate our children's reactions and dig deeper to find out WHY a particular event or experience is a trigger for them.

Some common empathy phrases I like to use are:

- "I see you are upset"
- "It seems like this is something your body doesn't like"
- "I can see you are uncomfortable"
- "It looks like you don't like this"

While these phrases might not describe how you feel about your child's reaction in the moment, that isn't important at this time. There will be time later for you to state your opinion, give suggestions, and guide the child, but that time has to come after the wall goes down. Empathy is the quickest way to get that wall down and allow you to stand alongside your child through the process of solving the problem together.

So next time your child comes to you with his wall up, arms crossed, brows furrowed, and ready to stand his ground, you will know the best way to respond is NOT with swift punishments or by trying to push through his wall. Instead you'll use empathy so he will bring that wall down himself, and together the two of you can work through the situation.

Put It Into Practice

1. List common situations or environments in which your child puts up walls. Look for common threads to discover exactly what skill your child is lacking or which sensory experience is prompting that wall to be put up.

2. Come up with 3-4 empathy phrases that you would like to try with your child in a moment of stress, tantrum, or withdrawal. Write them down, place them in a spot you can see them often, and use them at the first sign of problematic behavior.

Chapter Seven

LIVE TOGETHER, LAUGH OFTEN

After dealing with explosive, and what felt like constant tantrums, meltdowns, and arguments in my home for so long, I found myself conditioned to do something that ended up being very damaging for my family. During quiet times, I'd take the time to distance myself from my kids, take a deep breath, and do my chores or anything I could think of to get away from the kids. It was my way of staying sane, keeping my head above water, and finding a break in the quiet moments.

What started out as a survival skill for me, ended up as a way for me to always get away from my kids any chance I could get. Even when I would go places with them, I wasn't really with them. At the park while they played, I'd chat with a friend or scroll social media. At home, they'd do their thing and I'd do mine. We lived in the same home, but in completely separate worlds.

Sure, I was going through the motions of reading books to my kids at night, sitting down to dinner together, and doing other things that seemed like I was being with my kids. But on the inside, I was distant and completely disconnected. They caused chaos I couldn't deal with, so I distanced myself from them. I was hanging on by a thread and struggling to catch any break I could.

That wasn't a highlight in my parenting life, and writing those words now hurts my heart, but in all honesty, when things start to get crazy again, I find myself drifting back to that disconnected state.

At the peak of this time of chaos, I remember sitting on the couch of my counselor's office, feeling like a broken failure, and clueless about what to do. She asked a simple question that has stuck with me ever since; "What is the one thing you want most right now?" My answer? "Alone time, time away." I just wanted to escape. During that time there was no laughing. I wasn't truly living together with my kids, I was existing alongside of them.

While that answer was true then, I find the opposite to be true today. That all changed when my mindset changed. Instead of interacting with my kids only during times of chaos, crisis, and tantrums, I started making it a point to laugh with them every day, and truly live our lives together. Every single day. I've found that laughter only comes when I'm connected, living with my kids, interacting with them, and paying attention to them. Laughter is my goal every day now.

Our park days are no longer times for me to just chat with friends and ignore my kids. Instead, I take trips to the park with JUST my kids, I put my phone down, and interact with them. When I'm truly present with them, we laugh, we play, we bond. Those moments of happiness fill my soul with exactly what I need, and in turn, fill theirs too. It's no surprise, when we have times like this, the tantrums in our home decrease as well.

Amy McCready, author of The Me, Me, Me, Epidemic, calls this "mind, body, and soul time" and recommends parents make time for it daily. When parents and kids feel connected in their minds, bodies, and souls, there's a tangible change that happens. She suggests this time is the most important tool a parent can use to decrease whining, sulking, and pouting behaviors. Attention getting behaviors like those mentioned happen because a child doesn't feel heard or seen. When they feel heard and seen in positive ways, that need to act out diminishes.

In my home, that shift from wanting to fill my heart with time away from my kids, to filling my heart WITH my kids made all the difference in the world. That shift has changed my life, and the life of my kids as well.

When tantrums start creeping in, whining ramps up, and more bickering starts to occur, I can always trace it back to not having enough time truly living together, laughing, and listening to each other.

How to Make It Work

I know life is busy. Everyone can attest to that. With kids in the mix, it is even busier. We have soccer, t-ball, church, friends, homework, vacations, family, and SO MUCH MORE. It often feels like we can't add even one more thing.

A dear friend of mine once told me, "If we're always trying to FIND the balance, it will never happen. We have to CREATE it." With that in mind, I started creating time to live and laugh with my kids daily. Amy McCready suggests that each child should receive at least five minutes of uninterrupted time and attention from each parent every day. During this time, a parent should prepare to be completely present mentally and physically.

This is the model I used to turn things around in my home. I try to make this time as child-directed as possible. It is a time for me to listen, connect, and support my children physically and emotionally. I'll be honest, it doesn't come easy for me. Let me share a few tips that I have used to incorporate this "child-time" each day, realizing that what works for me won't work for everyone.

Personally, I like to spend a few minutes with each child in the morning when they first wake up and then again in the evening before bed. During our morning connection time I hold my kids, I talk about the day ahead, and basically just listen. By building in a brief talk about the day I give my kids the opportunity to prepare their bodies and minds for what will happen that day, which creates predictability and a sense of power for them. At night I do the same thing, giving gentle reminders of the events of the next day, asking a few open-ended questions and seeing where the conversation goes.

During the day they inevitably each come up to me with a request to do something with them. I try as often as possible to say yes. Typically, my own chores, social media, and all other things I spend my time doing, can wait. When I push other things aside and make my kids a priority, we all benefit. My kids don't necessarily know why I do it or even that it is part of our routine, but they have come to expect it.

One day, a particularly hard week of teasing, arguments, and bickering, my ten-year-old said, "Mom, can you promise to come give me a hug every night, even if I'm mad at you?" Even at his age, he has come to expect that live, laugh, listen time we usually have. During his tough week I had unintentionally distanced myself, and he noticed it. After that night of snuggles, things started to change the next day. For him and for me.

Ironically, I have found that I need that morning and evening connection time as well. When I start my day holding and loving each of my kids, I focus first on them. I fill my love bucket and am better prepared for whatever may come our way. Doing the same each evening, ending with positive and loving moments with them, helps me sleep better and feel like I ended the day on a good note.

Whatever ideas for live, laugh, and listen time may work for you and your family, be sure to make it part of your daily routine.

Put It Into Practice

1. Make a list of things you can you do to add "live, laugh, and listen" time into your day.

Chapter Eight

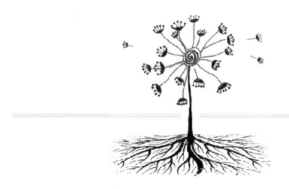

SOLVE PROBLEMS TOGETHER

*I*n the situations I've recounted, baseball practice, my son throwing a fit in church over the markers, his refusal to go outside, and countless others, you can see how we uncovered the root of the problem, but the next logical question is "then what?" A weed doesn't disappear the minute the roots are discovered. It takes one final step and a few PULLS to get that weed out effectively. That final step of actually solving the problem is the culminating event in this entire process.

If I had shared power, provided understanding, lowered the walls, and taken the time to laugh with my son before his baseball practice, but then jumped right into solving his problem by dishing out a solution _for_ him, I would have missed an important opportunity to teach one of the most important skills that caused the situation in the first place; his inability at that point in time to solve his own problems.

This final step is easy to skip, because we are all in the habit of telling our kids what to do, how to do it, and when it should be done. Waiting for them to come up with a reasonable and logical solution on their own is like taking the time to have a child vacuum the living room. It takes more work and more time than actually doing it yourself, but in the process, your child is able to practice a crucial skill that will serve her well the rest of her life.

The way each childhood problem is solved will teach a child something about how to navigate problems in the future, so it is important for you as a parent or caregiver to help the child reach a satisfying resolution that works for everyone.

During the situation with my son at church, when we reached the point of coming to a solution, his initial solutions weren't acceptable. This is normal for most kids as they are learning a skill, which takes time, practice, and mistakes. For instance, learning to ride a bike without training wheels doesn't usually happen overnight or on the first try. Kids need an adult holding the seat, giving gentle verbal guidance, support, and encouragement and a lot of falls, before they are able to take off riding on their own.

Learning to solve problems is the same. It's messy sometimes. It takes time, it takes practice and a lot of patience, BUT in the end, having a child who knows how to identify the problem and find an acceptable solution is worth all the work in the world.

While my son and I were in a private room far away from the chapel, I went through the PULLS process with him. When we reached the point of solving the problem, his initial solutions were: "I'm just going to go back out there and take her markers so I can have a full case," and "She just needs to give me all her markers or she will go to timeout for not sharing."

In situations like these when the solutions aren't feasible or acceptable (which will be the case with most proposed solutions), it's important to help the child see all the different sides of the story. Naturally kids are self-centered. They think mostly of themselves and their own happiness. Thinking outside themselves is a skill, that can be taught during this final step of solving the problem together. Henry Cloud and John Townsend, authors of the book Boundaries, teach that this is a crucial element for raising kids who can empathize, see outside themselves, and avoid a self-centered life.

So, as we sat in the room, I listened to my son spout off self-centered solutions. I would validate his effort, then I'd provide an understanding of the side he was missing: his sister's. I said things like, "Well, that could work for you, but how would your sister feel if she had two fewer markers?" or "I can see how that would help you, but that doesn't seem fair to your sister." Gently pointing out the side he wasn't able to see on his own helped him to think outside himself. Slowly but surely, with this guidance, he was able to reach a solution that worked for him, his sister, and the rest of the congregation, who just wanted to have a peaceful church session.

It would have been easy and a lot quicker to cut that weed down, solve the problem myself, and move on. In doing that, we would have left the roots- the inability to find solutions to his problems- still in the ground, ready to sprout another weed at any moment. Only by using the PULLS method will these tantrums start to decrease and stay away longer. It may not always look pretty, but in the end, it works like a charm.

Chapter Nine

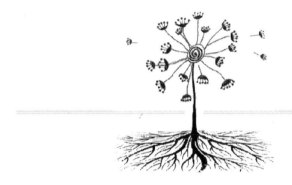

CONSEQUENCES AND DISCIPLINE

J'm the first to admit that my parenting is not perfect. I mess up almost every day, some days more than others. I used to feel that "messing up" meant "failing", but life has taught me otherwise.

When I find myself giving in to my short temper, saying something mean, or losing my patience with my kids, I take those moments to put myself through the PULLS process, search for the roots to my own weeds, and see where I need to try something different.

After I've found and analyzed the root of my own behavior, I make it a point to discuss it with my kids. Taking them through this not only gives them insight into their own behavior, but also provides a powerful, real-life example. They see me mess up, they see me apologize, they see me trying to be better every day. I feel it creates a sense of unity in our family. Nobody is above mistakes. Nobody is above apologies. And we are all in this together.

Natural Consequences

There are times my kids mess up too, and sometimes the mess is more than I'd like to deal with, but such is life. We live and then we get to learn. Growing up, I thought kids had to learn through punishment. When I would hit my brother, my dad would spank me for it every time. That never worked. What I learned was how to hit my brother and not get caught, hence escaping any punishment.

While many of us have been taught that punishment is the best teaching tool in parenting, most research states otherwise.

Shefali Tsabary says

> We've been so schooled to impose "lessons" on our children that it feels counterintuitive to allow the lesson to emerge naturally out of the situation.

> Moving away from discipline [or control] requires us to learn how to allow natural consequences to correct a child's behavior.

> Only when a child feels the consequence of their behavior do they get the message. If we impose a penalty, they don't get the message-they simply resent us.

> There are natural consequences to all behavior--positive or negative results that either improve the quality of our everyday lives or make life more difficult. To allow natural consequences

to take their course is in no way punitive, but simply a necessary part of helping a child grow up.

Natural consequences are usually more effective than artificial ones. A child who chooses not to clean her room will have a hard time finding clean clothes after about a week. A kid who decides not to pick up toys in the playroom might later find some of the toys to be broken or missing. A kid who chooses to dress in summer clothes during the cool fall months will inevitably feel cold at some point in the day. Those consequences can't be avoided. They are inevitable and powerful.

Allowing those consequences to happen is not an easy task for parents, because we have a tendency to want to shield and protect our kids from any harm, discomfort, or negative consequences. We don't want our kids to get cold, so we argue with them about wearing a jacket in the morning. We don't want our kids to be late to school so we nag them all through the morning routine then leave the house on time, but frustrated, every morning. We make kids sit at the dinner table until they finish the portion of food we decided they need to eat, because we are afraid they might eventually get hungry.

Those are the moments we don't allow natural consequences to set in. Those are also the moments that exhaust us, wear us down, and make us want to give up. We can't possibly fight every battle throughout the day.

The solution is to choose your battles wisely, focusing only on those things that can't be settled through natural consequences.

The amount of control we assert control over our children is a personal choice. The more we control, the less they are able to learn and experience on their own. Allowing the opportunity for children to learn, think, and grow alongside us through experiencing natural consequences is the most powerful way to help them learn those lessons.

Chapter Ten

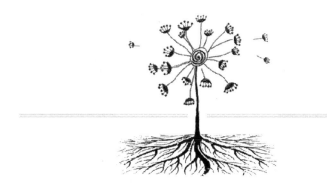

EMBRACE THE IMPERFECTIONS

*J*ust as Ross Greene states, kids do well when they CAN. The concepts in this book outline ways for you to support your child so they CAN do their absolute best at any given moment.

As we take small daily steps to support, encourage, and educate our children, we will see a shift in their behaviors. What was once a wall of defiance, stubbornness, and refusal will turn into a conversation about what is happening inside, and a cooperative process of finding a solution together without the screaming, power struggles, or tears that once existed. Statements and demands will slowly turn into more questions, and those defiant tendencies from your child will turn into more cooperative action. The changes happen gradually as you work with your children to foster the support and guidance they need.

The road won't be perfect. Being in the garden, pulling weeds out by the roots, stirs up a lot of dirt. It gets messy sometimes. There will be missteps, there will be hard falls, but now you have the tools to know exactly why the behavior is happening and how to address it most effectively.

Even the most incredible garden will produce a weed every now and then. Guiding your child towards better behavior is a constant process, but it doesn't have to be the constant grueling uphill battle we all have experienced. Nor do we as parents have to look like the social media image constantly in front of us, dictating what motherhood should look like.

Each of us has an image of the parent we originally wanted to be. That picture will come back into focus as you use the PULLS method of the behavior weeds you see in your home. That picture, no matter how plain or simple it may be, will fill your heart and soul with more joy than any fake social media image ever will. I can attest to that each time I look at my kids now, hearing them talk about their feelings and problems, and walking alongside them as they learn to navigate the ups and downs this life has to offer.

It's a beautiful ride; we might as well enjoy it.

All my best,

Wendy

REFERENCES

Cloud, Dr. Henry. *Boundaries.* Grand Rapids: Zondervan, 1992. Print.

Greene, Ross W. *The Explosive Child.* New York: Harper & Row, 1999. Print.

Katie, Byron. *Loving What Is.* P.3

Mc Cready, Amy. Positive Parenting Solutions.

Tobias, Cynthia. You Can't Make Me But I Can Be Persuaded.

Tsabary, Shafali. Out of Control.

Voss, Angie. ASensoryLife.com

email for details:
info@WendyBertagnole.com

PARENTING
COACH & WORKSHOPS

wendy bertagnole
Imperfect Mom

EVERYDAY SOLUTIONS FOR CHALLENGING BEHAVOIR

WendyBertagnole.com

93867399R00042

Made in the USA
Lexington, KY
19 July 2018